"Eric Forsbergh has produced a rich and varied collection of poetry that showcases the versatility of his talent. He begins with an underlying theme of the biological basis of our uniqueness and expands into the societal and spiritual ties that bind us in our humanity. He gives us poetry of science, poetry of love and war, and poetry of life and death. I am grateful to have shared his poetic journey and look forward to future creations."

—JILL CONLEY, president and CEO, Global Health, Education, and Research Solutions

"Who would have thought that poems about DNA could be made, by turns, whimsical, contemplative, witty, moving, and funny? Eric Forsbergh's poems are all these. And these poems breathe, with intimacy and longing, like conversations among old friends."

—JOHN Y. LEE, academic dean, John Leland Center for Theological Studies

"In his masterful *This Mortal Coil*, Eric Forsbergh explores human heredity in narrative poems that surprise and delight with unexpected images. In 'Rockport Graves,' for example, Forsbergh writes of 'two buried wives' who 'cannot realize how eternity, / like fanning out a hand of cards, / expands like an accordion.' Drugs, war, love, even lobstering—the poet takes a wide look at life to suggest why we are who we are and why that matters."

—SALLY ZAKARIYA, author of *All Alive Together*

This Mortal Coil

This Mortal Coil

Poems of DNA

ERIC FORSBERGH

RESOURCE *Publications* • Eugene, Oregon

THIS MORTAL COIL
Poems of DNA

Resource Publications
An Imprint of Wipf and Stock Publishers
199 W. 8th Ave., Suite 3
Eugene, OR 97401

www.wipfandstock.com

PAPERBACK ISBN: 978-1-6667-8832-7
HARDCOVER ISBN: 978-1-6667-8833-4
EBOOK ISBN: 978-1-6667-8834-1

VERSION NUMBER 09/18/23

Contents

Consequence I

Consequence II

Sequence I

After My Cousin Posted Her DNA

A half-sister of yours surfaces.
A Janice, sixty-eight, and older
than you not by much.
Her mother? A Myrtle
who died one recent year
one highway exit west.

The stitchwork fits.
A tartan plaid but more precise:
your father's cloth.

Thirty years too late to ask.

An unexpected slant
of light filters into
every room of every house
you lived in as a child. Again
you watch him after dinner
light a second cigarette.
You step into the smoke
but the kitchen dissipates

into an unknown room,
two greenish mirrors face-to-face
layering away like years.
Except for you and her,
both in motion, inside
two endless corridors of want.

3

Aching for an Oracle

Because uncertain fates suspend themselves
like clouds that lace a mountain,
while you, alert, are carried
toward some hinged event
—war, haj, the push of childbirth—
you wake up aching for an Oracle.

You'll find Her sitting on a tripod at Delphi
spent from a ritual frenzy
inhaling vapors from a mountain cleft.
You cannot question or address.
The scribe translates Her murmurs
in exchange for sacrifice.
Her cryptic utterance leaves
the sense of snakes inside your tunic.
Your children are statues, clammy with sweat.
When darkness clots, you
travel home alone.

Now, no need to pack.
Logan Airport's snowed in anyway.
Oracles inhabit every fiber of your being:
You just mail off your spit.
A lab will tease genetic fibers out,
predicting Parkinson's, Alzheimer's, et al.
The gamut as a gauntlet.
Predestination latches to your skin
under your flowing yoga top.

And you may find yourself wishing for
the indistinct voice of a Priestess
moaning from a chair.

Zipper

Because you asked what route this was
as he stood waiting for a bus,
sunset enveloping his head,
and his manner piqued your interest, this
led you to find him once again
to impress your smile
in his memory's clay.
Two months later he waits quietly
in the dark as you slowly unzip
yourself and three years later
you are pregnant.
                    You are reminded of
that winter in Genetics seminar, how
chromosomes unzip and now
yours and his clasp into someone
by now the size of a walnut,
this half-and-half agreement, so far
your blood-and-flesh imaginary friend.

Animal Husbandry

That's intercourse!
proclaims my mother, voice
amplified off the barn.
I cringe, at ten, but give no sign.

Gone, the immature conceptions.
Laid out flat as a shadow.
In the barnyard glare,
I watch almost a ton
mount the cow, his haunches juddering.

Rut did not appear to me in Sunday School, when,
balanced in companionable nakedness,
Adam drew the apple from the open palm of Eve.

And down off Deep Spring Hollow Road,
that fifth-grade girl I admire?
Will she witness her father hobble their cow?
Can his softened speech assuage the startle in her eyes?
What lies inside the way a family talks?

Our household terms confirmed themselves
one evening after several years.
As I plugged away at high school chemistry,
papers lapping the kitchen table,
I heard my younger sister's slippers
slapping down the hall.
Mom! Mom! I'm in heat!

After Watching the History Channel with You

Design bends history.
Viking longboats hewn for raid and rape.
In salt, a stable keel to plow resistant swells.
In fresh, a shallow draft to ply a river's reach.
Laden home, they cast among themselves
for human sacrifice. In nines. Only males.
Slit. Then hung in Odin's holy grove.

A Swedish air clings to my name.
Every syllable. Me, a leaf
of temperance, of democratic socialist.

Across the couch, you stir again,
fingering your printed DNA results.
You'd lilted in telling of the Celtic tale,
chanted through with Cherokee.
Such chorus bearing on its back
your thread of song.

I remember how, last month,
you spat your strands
into a cup. Screwed down the lid.
Buried it in the mailbox, raising the red flag.

Tuesday, in a twist,
your chromosomes unraveled your narrative.

You, anew: a swipe of Scandinavian.
A forced entry to your house of myth?
The rest a rinse, a Northern European mix,
Iberia abiding in your eyes.

How do you rebut your blood?
Do all threads of DNA
become a chain of ancestors?

And might you and I eye that one blonde axman
as the sparrow did? After breaching surf,
he adjusts his helmet, unsheathes his blade,
and lopes off toward the nearest hut.

The Police Will Swab Your Cheek

You: encyclopedia of binaries.
Off-On.   On-Off.   Zero-One.

Swabbed, your DNA surrenders to the decoding gauntlet.
How many couples make a you?

Thymine-Adenine. Cytosine-Guanine.
Guanine-Cytosine. Adenine-Thymine.

Three billion base pairs ladder up anyone's identity.
In cloud banks of windowless buildings,

you're shelved like rolls of patterned wallpaper
to be scrolled down, to be read: enough slight

variation to excise you from your tribe.
Police will tell you choice is binary, so during

a street demonstration, your image gets combed out.
Blizzards of pixels cull your cross-referenced face

from the anthem crowd. Bent,
                              you clutch your head
to buffer another gauntlet. Truncheons

economize interrogation. Confession is relief
for everyone. Truth. Lie. On. Off.

Binary, you cried at birth. Your four base pairs swarm,
jostle into line along a billions loaded spool

composing you: more musical chairs than
music of the spheres, circling from the time

of Socrates. He too thought at a tangent to authority.
Calm or not, he drank the state's solution.

Struck,
        your ears ring in a spinning orbit slowed by
    hands grabbing for the walls.

Blackness yanks a sack over your head.
Your carcass bounces once against the floor.

Hanging by a Thread

Over the countertop
between the microwave and fridge,
she leans to spit
into a screw-tight plastic cup,
DNA hanging by a thread.

Hung with documents, a tree
had grown from her computer screen.
Birth. Race. Death. Race. Port of entry. Race.
So far, an Irish tale. A story of sod
furrowed up like pages in the earth:
typhoid, flood, death by childbirth,
by ax, gun, boat, chain, log, horse.

Until the word *mulatto* launched off the page:
a census record, 1810, Virginia's shore.

She spits with purpose.
Hopes to tell what truth
may rupture out of truth-be-told.
Perhaps to watch
her knob-knock uncle punch the wall.

That night, through the ceiling,
she dreams about a constant brow of clouds
sifted by savannah grass
rising off a tan continent of hills,
and she sees
a beaded Tswana bride,

brass loops lengthening her neck,
emerge from the preparation hut,
a symmetry of self.

On a Surgeon Poet

A wound on paper isn't quite a wound.
It's a distant diagnosis, lying on clean sheets,
no seeps or stains, untreatable, a page unanswered

while in the moment I confer with Mr. Abdi,
who shifts his weight to parry pain
when the nib becomes a knife.

They say reflection-action alternates:
A metronome seeks symmetry either way.
Some schools of medicine are introducing

verse, tempering the old vice-versa: the need to
operate or not. A new contemplation in a new
sequestered space. First, listen to the patient. Balance

every phrase, and how the pauses weigh. Follow
the mouth trying to translate for the eyes. Observe
the aging face plowed under by its grievances. All poetry.

Saturdays, in the belly of a bookstore, it's me and words.
When one darts me from an unexpected angle, I suck in my breath.
Already sitting, I shrink myself enough to slip inside a sorrow

fragile as a sparrow, or into a brittle tuft of radiated hair, or
someone else's final lover, or the skin's gray paste of kidney failure,
perhaps a whitewashed family, or an old Somali castigating death.

But by Sunday afternoon, my eyes begin to flit and skim
along a line that tries to lead me on: a track across
an endless field of snow. And I miss the imperative of blood.

A Neat Trick If You Can

With both eyes open
it's a neat trick if you can, you say.

To see with one eye through a microscope
while drawing microbes through the other eye.
I try and fail half the afternoon.

Your phase-contrast world swims and flagellates,
caught between a glass slide and a cover slip.

With the delicacy of making love
your off-hand coaxes knurled knobs,
shifting your mobile stage,
finding focus where you wish,
as your dominant hand draws,
pencil to a pad.

Can your brain straddle that gap, you ask,
when one becomes the other?

While growing up, you practiced it
on your mother as you watched her
down the hallway from your room.
You told me so.
You sketched your life,
even posing in the mirror
with her stolen cigarette
though you've never smoked a day.

Meditation on Gregor Mendel

The river hushes past outside the wall.
Monastic practice rises to knead loaves
as Mendel tends his plants in muted prayer:
a rising silver fish, a silent call.

So often we invite disturbances.
The oxen bellow in the town below,
markets clattering with trade, and butchers
hanging swine and goats, gutted high to low.

Small thoughts blossom to larger principles
sometimes. His walled off garden of the mind,
with muffled hoeing, can allow a kind
of active animal to thrive inside.

His rows are columned, linear, each plant
recorded, numbered like accountants' books.
Quietly, he'll neuter eugenics' cant
of children bred for purity: with peas.

The stamens snipped, he paints on pollen dust
in silent labor, so every plant must
bloom his line. We, and peas, grow parallels:
white or purple, tall or short, smooth or rough,

green or yellow. He's fetched God's master key:
the gene. Fresh tendrils bending, bowing, toward
the sun, Mendel amends the loam with care.
Between each row, he hoes a space for prayer.

To the Next Cold Case Killer

The unlikely crime-fighter cracking decades-old murders?
A genealogist.

Washington Post, July 22, 2018

When the milk eye of the moon is blind
to everyone but you,

when the raccoon in your garbage can
is Sergeant Lou collecting the cup
he saw you drinking from,

when you're caged inside the story of
the California Killer on a chain,

when your brother, and your cousin, reveal
themselves online, pre-occupied, not noticing
you match their height, hair, and ethnic mix,

when your curtains breathe open on their own,

when you won't look up at night, because
the Pleiades sear pinholes in your retinas,

and when you're startled by the shape of
a shark, a darkened cruiser easing down your street,

when sweat drips like tracer bullets
to illuminate your every bruise, under
a scaffold sky of black and blue,

just when, after twenty-seven years, you thought
you're free and clear, the DA's filed for arrest.
She's strung up your DNA.

To You, Mary Shelley

The gift offered is different for each,
but all are equal in their grandeur.

Lyanda Lynn Haupt

Mary Shelley?
About your Frankenstein.
A monster?
Cursed. Gawp-mouthed.
In pain. From parts.

The book itself is the mutation.
Who else's hand could leave
these cursive fingerprints?

Your brain at driven play:
gestalt encompassing gestalt,
electricity in chains.
Sudden? Often.
Normal? Never.
Always, always
toward mutation.

Do you conceive it
as Saint Elmo's Fire
on the fingertips?

Or do you stitch, unstitch, re-stitch
into a softened stop,
half-asleep by candlelight.

Mary, do you startle
from a nightly grave
when a lightning strike
sets fire to a line?

How often does a page
breathe without warning
in the dark?

Gene Silencing

Somehow, the Twin Towers crossed my mind today:
that mountains could collapse.
Girders plunging, skewering the subways.
Ten-foot panes exploding on the pavement.

Three thousand dead,
                as I recalled my grandmother at length
curled up cursing, rasping at me not to talk

as carcinoma multiplied the knuckles of
its fingers, choking her intestines.

All this, pre-morphine-lollipops as well.

24 thousand genes grew her to fruition.
But a lone wolf mutated in her colon
and led to a metastasis of caliphates.

Like an Al Qaeda operative,
the silenced gene now lies
darted with an siRNA,
barely breathing,
a black sack on its head.
Can that gene cough up encryptions for
tens of thousands dead?

At times, I saunter avenues of memory.
Every cluster of events resides
inside a shop, each with an attenuated light:

gin rummy played into the night,
the way she squeezed my cheek
when she approved of my new girl,
textures of her borscht.

Even now, recollections
stagger the streets, embedded
by her shattered glass of agonies.

Even now I feel her
fingernails dig into my wrist.

First, the Good News

*Whole-genome sequencing of newborn babies
presents ethical quandaries.*

THE ECONOMIST, MAY 2022

You're going to have a baby.
You've wanted one since
the two of you fell in love
with your custom rework
of an epic narrative:
Odysseus drags himself, bloodied, from the surf.
Athena, gray-eyed, wraps him in an unguent fog
and gifts him to a curious Penelope.
Aren't new lovers the heroes of their tales?

Next, your lineage, your Telemachus,
arrives, sprung from
the lime-colored grass of a spring afternoon.
But did you consult the prophets first?

Some 7,000 rare diseases lie in wait,
a Trojan army out beyond the plain.
All genetic. All in battle garb,
dark eyes restless
through their helmet slits.
One is all it takes.

Pay enough, and
the seers tell you everything.

The new Cassandra
predicts entirely
the issue of your loins.
An office consultation looms
in which you hope she won't keen
in a bloodshot voice.

Now, no one can dismiss such a figure,
so robed in utter potency.

That Punk Look

Years—and randomly—we
chat down at the coffee shop,
and years she thwarts
the blonde grain.

She flaunts two sleeves
of riot ink, black hair
an Oklahoma flat-top.
She revels in her studs,
tiny steel ones,
the two competing
for her lip and tongue.
No pearls in either ear,
gems and rings rim
her soft oyster shells.
I comment on
her earlobes punch-holed
into exclamation points.
In April, she flashes me
new script which corrugates
its way down her ribs.

Summer drifts lightly,
empty of her weight.

In September,
looking freshly stapled on,
a block letter tattoo
against the back half

of her cranium:
CHALLENGE ACCEPTED.
The skin's too smooth,
no stubble left, no follicles.
She rubs her head.
Check this out.
The look's completed
by my chemotherapy.

Raining Diamonds

On Neptune, scientists forecast rainstorms of solid diamonds.
JOURNAL NATURE ASTROPHYSICS

Raise your hand to block what's on the way.
Allow your brain   to take a breath   to quell your
vertigo.   Eclipse?   Your thumb can blot the moon
which blots the sun.
                Did ancients fear some darkening eye of God?
And you? Did you wring design from what aligned?

Consider self.   Our DNA contains
                snippets from viruses, bacteria,
pre-amphibians,   and Neanderthals:
yards of yarn with frays of lint.   All, crumbs along a trail.

Our helix also bears the scatterings   of empty beach,
of nonsense DNA.   Nonsense.   Until it's not.
Science grinds and sorts.
Impeccable, its brutal rationale.

Bubbled in a matrix   between atoms and cosmos,
we barely grasp.   We flounder around the gaps.
        Do we just gabble on in earth's peculiar dialects?
Marie Curie saw through us. Just bare bones.

Any moment   a memory blinks awake   each one
its own synaptic chain along electric cells.
Meanwhile   any new odor gets attached

to   one   nerve ending in the nose. Gleeful then,
        we huddle in the memory of smell.

Underground oceans of water frequent the   moons
of Jupiter, ripe for life.   We've learned this now.
Gaseous   jets erupt out of their poles.

Any gene CRISPR edits a better you
        before   your coffee break.
Metaphor begins to slip.   We lose our grip.

You and I met on the street last week. Call it chance.
No Baba's tale flew us in, riding on its back.

Einstein saw design.
God   or   not,   the self cradles narrative:
        the homemade doll you and I must fabricate.

As we dissect   the overarch   the underpinnings,
will we recoil from ourselves?

Is each of us a sack of random loves and tragedies
where chemistry and physics intersect?

The Neighborhood Neanderthal

Neanderthal gene found to reduce COVID-19
THE ECONOMIST

He hasn't always lived at this address,
merely 60,000 years or so.
He's on the twelfth chromosome,
up there by the bend, almost hard to find
inside this maze of avenues.
His gene resides in one spot.
It's like the 416 Shady Maple Place
of leafy dreams.

We found him in his yard today,
busy touching up a gravel path
to all the neighbor's homes.
We appreciate his evening walk,
his dawn patrol.
When feral dogs invade our street,
he lugs his shotgun out,
splattering their brains
across the well-kept lawns
while we peer
out of our windows in relief.

Some say he wears a surly look.
We've heard the cruel remarks:
the sloped forehead,
the heavy brow of bone

above the eyes. To the vigilantes
of the neighborhood,
his gait seems awfully suspicious.
But, damn, he's kept the beasts at bay.

Axolotl

Compared to the axolotl,
a foot or so of Mexican salamander,
we tower in our mastery. Yet

the axolotl packs DNA in tenfold quantity
to you and me. If only we could flourish
half its tricks. It regrows severed limbs.

Stressed, it stages metamorphosis.
Surgically implanted with a third eye,
in time, the axolotl gives it sight.

As a boy, I feared the neighbor soldier
home on leave, for what he did to me.
Recollection's bed contorts into a rack.

Each memory is just another protein chain.
Could a surgeon release us into freedom?
Could she amputate a memory by cyberknife?

We'd end up like the axolotl, recovering
while a healthy stump of memory
regrows, fresh and newly pink.

What the Eye Perceives

Rosalind Franklin, 1952

Breeze feathers the lake. Aloft,
an eagle scans, rising on the thermals.
All fixed eye. All pursuit
of quarry lazing into sight: a fish.
Its green back shaped like yes. Or no.

An English biophysicist hunches over,
adjusts a microscope's knob.
Her focal range scans another
fresh expanse, a glass slide
whose flotsam shifts its shapes
in something like a lake below.
Anticipation dries her mouth.

Unstrung proteins waft like water weeds.
Among waves, minnows, cell shreds,
a small fry of mitochondrial debris,
a turtle's back, ruptured nuclei, frogs,
the eye perceives. The eagle,
in a sharp turn, dives.

Franklin's lab captures photo 51,
DNA as pure geometry:
our diagram.
A folded tight infinity.
Stranger to the world than
microscopic Cubist origami.

Falling Asleep

A sudden twitch as you begin to drift.
It's quick. Sometimes with a frisson of fear
about to plummet from a cliff.

It too has a name, known to few,
but nameless it remains to most of us.

Will you conclude it was intrusions of a dream?
A lucent wave burst against
a headboard, the perimeter of bedposts
marking off the architecture in the room?

Or a replay of that moment when
your older brother halfway slipped
gripping your hand down in that dim well,
while your dad, deaf and unaware,
forever rounds the barn?

Perhaps a synapse snapping off
after thirty years, the memory of a lover,
each of you a shadow spent,
now on your own side of another bed?

Or, by its truest name,
hypnagogic myoclonus passing through,
broaching on a terror as you age:
encroaching loss of self-control.

34

Or just your body practicing for death,
objecting one last time
to letting go?

The Gene Named FOXP2

Our family camps at a kitchen table yammer fest. Our door is always open
and Reggie's gone for beer. Hands at cards, our mouths run free, as the lamp
pools on Leigh Anne with her soprano, on Tuan debating anything.

FOXP2 acts out the only turnstile through which each builder on the way
to Babel fits, hoisting hods of rock, adobe, brick. Paths, tunnels, viaducts
interlace with Escher's flying stairs: shortcuts our family invents

to mine this mountain for gems of slang we hang
along our chain of narrative. You remember the one
about Lakshmi shaming the delivery boy? How

she laid her consonants down, mouth clicks
crisp as billiard balls? And by the way, which linguist
gave a speech on ululations and the fluttering of tongues?

Aditya, did you call your husband out? Did we show the love by
laughing, Mahdi, as you mimicked birds of Ethiopia? And Koharu,
to watch you wrangle that boiling-over thought

from stove to countertop by the handle of its word. Even busboys
wield the subjunctive: woulda, coulda, shoulda. Except
Reggie, who prayed out loud to bring his new wife back

from Vietnam, the years it took to mold his mouth around her
mother tongue because she loved that Reggie first and last
when no one else had ever spoken up for him.

Sequence II

AJ and the Chipper

A mangler for sure, and it's all hers.
Gulps branches, shrubs, brush, metastasizing roots.
Spews chips at high speed. A rattle growl pounding air.
Now past breast cancer, her strength
again jacks up the welded bell mouth.

She reconnects to sense of smell in clouds
of cedar shreds. Sweat sparkles from her earlobes,
diamondlike. It streaks her farmwork walnut hands,
seeps along the crisscross threads of neckline tan.

She hauls that beast everywhere,
iron-posted to her tractor hitch. To the neighbors.
Up the lane. Past the ruminant cattle.
She grins *I'll mulch your top field, Frank.*
I need three oak timbers from you anyway.

By the time the sun drops pace,
her chipper squats in the dark barn, steel greased to go.

Across a shorn lawn, sunset claws of trees
insinuate toward the bright house.
Striding in, she pulls the front door tight against the latch.

Under the Influence of Internet

     Calf deep through roiling surf
I wade.   Elsewhere, fixated millions   plash in electron's froth as
well.
     Opaque foam bursts against my legs, pippling away as evanescent lace.

*I reach out with a lurch.   Shoes!   They hover, almost dancing,
       retreating backwards on their toes, a coy come-on.   My size   My style*

I thrash my legs a little harder yet.   Keep up keep up.

My mind tacks, stumbling backwards onto last night.
     In half-sleep, had I presumed to scan in Alighieri's hand?

Virgil admonished Dante on the cliff
to plant his/ My attention frays then snaps. /heels on each descending stone.

    Abrupt.   Swifter shoes catch my eye like a sweater brushing across a nail.

    A few gluey strands of kelp in brownish rot
       wrap around my knees, beseeching me, then slither off.

Waves in tumults   Random specks of light   Bubbled curling surfaces.

As Virgil testified/   As Virgil/   I squib away from Virgil's train of thought,
                          but crimp my face to capture it again.
As Virgil testified, to Dante's shock,
"Those shrieking hogs flayed raw? The credit thieves."
                                 Back-lit baubles shimmy.
     Retreating waves scoop sand holes around my feet,

embedding them another inch.   I draw out with a sucking feel.

                              One special offer is Italian, hand-sewn, bespoke.
But another ten pairs of stamped-out gudge are priced
with ten more pairs at fifty percent off.
                              How do you box yourself? To be shipped out? Not free?

Plovers outrun claws of waves,
                         racing back to pick out sea-lice in the squirming sand.

     Will I try to swim toward deeper calm?
     Can I see the motionless sandy bottom, twenty feet below?
     Has my composure lost its/   stroke then breathe, stroke then breathe?

Any color desired? Even rainbow for the neoprene soles?   Gulls screech
close above.

Another box is laid at my front step
with a single doorbell ring and run, one of abandonment.

          I've adopted any attribute purchased by my enhanced self.

Surf sounds like static, like tinnitus. It drowns each complex harmony.

     Ankle highs or low-cuts?   *Cross-fit or basketball?*
       A textured surface pretends to lend the uppers depth.

With fourteen thousand lines,

               now Dante viewed the bowl of hell complete,
               as Virgil analyzed the scene in depth.
               The rocky path had bruised their legs and/

Cornucopia at pornographic scale.
     A million hands quiver as each approaches from behind to mount the
mouse.

41

Measuring the Bull

You have a lunch date all set up.
An outdoor café tablecloth,
dapples fluttering like curiosity
under a breezing tree.
You check your cell phone selfie face.

He asks your name
and reassured, he sits.
Shoulders, waist, hands, face.
You focus on the eyes and mouth,
the way they act around his narrative.
You size him up. It's normal.

The Angus Cattle Association's way ahead of you.

Every bull gets his genome strung out to
thousands of predictions:
pedigree, muscle mass,
appetite, fertility, and even
—though you may never care—
circumference of the scrotum.
In other words, when needed,
does he have the balls?

But something may occur to you.
What's behind his sudden narrowing of eyes?
Something you may regret about this date?

42

The Association's further down the road
than you could guess.
They've quantified the prize:
docility.
Well, you may not want to go that far.
You're not shopping for a pet.
Check one or more or none:
patient, kind, nurturing.
Could those be captured
and corralled?

Telomere

The tip on every chromosome

How many mornings more to roll from bed?
How many times to climb the hill?
And to be blunt,
how many soirees overstayed
before your body summons the disgust
to throw the book at you?

The telomere, a ticket taker,
collects a chit from every cell
on the toll road to replacement.
It keeps the time-table strict.
Barring intervention from the scheduler,
it decides when you leave the station
laid out in the mail car.
On time? Or well before?
It's known to be punctilious,
and tears off extra chits for strewing
garbage through your house.

Strolling leisurely along La Grande Jatte,
you want to lengthen out the count.
You whisper to the river, *Slow yourself.*
You invent an endless sunny day
to kiss someone you love. After all,
how efficient could those ticket-takers be?
Consider this a parallel: Each ten years
every ounce of bone you're hung upon,

spine, skull, scapula,
has been replaced.
Its chit-book spent, each
cell line in you dies.

In the beginning,
painted by a Pointillist,
now thrown into reverse,
you and I disappear by
dots.

The Unknown Soldiers of Shiloh Battlefield Park

I saw battle-corpses, myriads of them,
and the white skeletons of young men.

WALT WHITMAN

Past the one-room log church
in Shiloh Tennessee,
across peach orchards,
blossoms bursting apart carpeting the dirt,
across bogs and splintering trees,
across gullies overflowing with soldiers
wallowing in smoke, across hazy farms,
lead shot thickened the air so much
sometimes two bullets would collide, melding
into one the shape of a homunculus.
For thousands killed to a standstill in two days,
Grant paid escaped slaves
—when a Black man ranked as contraband—
half a wage to bury all of them.
1700 Confederates were laid like logs,
several deep in shallow trenches, names smothered
under mounds: low altars heaving up the land.
Pittsburg Landing, and another 1700 Union men,
where few stones arranged
in parade formation identify a name.

The night before Cold Harbor,
Grant's men pinned notes to their backs,

names penciled on. In the march for Richmond
they'd passed skulls scattered in the fields,
picked clean of chapter, verse and line
by maggots, birds and feral dogs.

For every war including Vietnam,
one unknown soldier
would be raised, and borne to Washington.
He who might have been our son
becomes our nation's faceless one.
Shot down on a bombing run above An Loc,
a candidate was duly found. In time,
a Missouri family matched the facts.
Genetic traces linger in the dense temporal bones,
unveiling First Lieutenant Blassie.
Afghanistan, and every soldier's genome
gets counted like a rosary. Now,
each seated wife or mother holds the folded flag,
uncertainty's black veil lifted
in light of who is known.

Free Heroin

The Swiss provide it.

Civil servants measure out
powder in a glassine pack.

A clean shooting gallery. A chaise.
A nurse to check the riddled pulse.
Not cut with talc, glass dust,
or powdered rust.

Vomit, and the high intensifies.

The state's the dealer now, so
fewer are coerced to start the trip.
Fewer far.

Yet once exposed, pleasure genes erupt
in crimson yellow purple blossoms
along tight stalks, hollyhocks of DNA,
then a slow wilt
into brownish pulps
at rehab intake:
    assist you not to nod at lunch,
    set a time for bed,
    give you a TV, a toilet,
    two tablets of an anti-drug.

Emptier now, treatment centers
erect fewer Babels of billable hours,

investors taking note.
Hieronymus Bosch was right.
Voyeurs seek the naked, pierced.

Without fresh flesh, Zurich gargoyles
scratch their famished guts,
thumb-lock their Glocks, scrape
their claws along the chapel gutters,
wolfing down their young.

First Sonogram

Seen from your upper
window, down the block
at some remove,
like an Edward Hopper black and white,
and grainy through the screen,
a streetlamp's cone
shines down. There,
you notice a figure,
indistinct, possibly familiar,
curled as if to tie a shoe.
And you wonder who it is.

Narcan

It looks appealing
dressed up as a nasal spray.
Designed in white, a little rocket ship
with a tip that, all the way,
reaches to the inside corner of the eye.

Harmless. Anyone can pocket it.
I bought it just to carry down
cracked and potted streets of anywhere.

Me,
nothing but a passerby.
You,
lying like a deer hit at the side of the road.
Or on a sidewalk,
collapsed like a mattress in a dump.

Lungs suffocating.
Retinas like pinholes.

If I can't jostle you awake
I'll root it up your nose and squeeze.
911, and all the wailing.
Why wouldn't I,
after what I see
our local medics do?

I'd like to get just one day back
with no one left for dead outside the wire.

Cyclone

A cyclone scours Mozambique.
Rivers roil, copper under hammered light.
Mudslides sluice villages into
swaths of cinder blocks. Cars protrude
like tilted tombstones of the local chiefs,
and bodies can be found by smell.

My friend Obal says, *You know us Africans.*
We blame it on the gods. I say the gods are innocent.

And of the One God?
Believers fear to look. Or look away.
From childhood, I learned to bow my head.

Or of the smaller gods? In the oak out front,
a pair of gods rummages a nest each year.
The woodpile cricket saws his god-like wings.
The chimney god even fools the cat.

Or a trickster god who plays a finger in the crumbs?
Crystals or crystal meth?

Consider the blood and tissue self.
Which dire gods might circulate,
fearsome in disease's tapestries?
Which therapeutic weapons do they dread,
held aloft by righteous Durga from her holy throne?

Godlike as well, which iotas of your genes
pounce and bound along your arteries,
nesting in your flesh?
How often do they sanctify the self?
Do they pulse inside the mouth?
Throb behind the eyes?

Their will is to procreate.
They have the fix on you.
And when your ears flush red
how briefly they admit you
to the tasting room of paradise.

Twice Identified as Eve

Agent Samuel, brother in faith, recalls it thus:

The heroin dealer moans from the takedown,
face-first on the bedroom floor,
hands cuffed behind for murder in another state.
Samuel and another federal agent stand over him.
A shard of light cuts through a torn shade.

Two back-up cops, beef in bullet-proof,
keep weapons drawn.
Everyone is Black in this abrupt tableau,
when justice like a river wants to flow.

In the middle of the room,
the interrupted girlfriend stands naked in a freeze of fear,
her fingers curled to small fists at her mouth,
her forearms trying to hide her breasts.
Her eyes flick man to man to man
as a cop calls for a woman officer. Meanwhile,

as only attending angels can, each burly agent
gently bends to pinch a corner of a sheet, stands,
and drapes her lightly into modesty, where she begins
to breathe of Nefertiti. They avert their eyes,
so cannot see the scattering of scars
and hot pan burn marks in semilunar clues.
The keloid on her neck?
This the agents miss, occupied in the arrest.

From beneath the sheet, what's rancid falls away from her
and she is as washed as a Black Madonna.

Nor, in her, do they notice either of the two Eves.
The anthropological Eve, found deep in a cave's recess
in the Eastern plains of Africa, her very bones
exposed in dirt. She. The gene of all our genes.
And the pristine Eve, born of the fruitful garden,
to whom God said *Who told you that you were naked?*

The Bible weighs out epic sagas, legal matters, poetry,
letters, philosophical reflection, and apocalyptic literature.
Hiding in its thickets, still the spotless girlfriend clutches at her sheet.

Smoldering

His white coat falling open,
Ajit leans forward, cradling my hand
as if to keep some gossamer of death
from separating us. *The first stage*
is known as smoldering.

I squint. Through
fifty years of Agent Orange residue,
I see the hills around Da Nang
without a blade of grass,
villages under drifting snakes
of burnt orange atmosphere.

No ambush ever waited longer.
Our own men
set the booby trap
and covered it with leaves.

Gobbets of my marrow churn out
protein dystopias.
My bones smolder
until I resent the very word.
It seeds my consciousness,
a parasite
that lays its eggs at night.

California's smoldering.
The working stiffs are smoldering.

On Ajit's wall, his sacred Punjab
smolders in a photograph.

Perhaps he holds my hand
to keep from going back.

To the COVID Health Care Workers

I expect to get the virus.

A NURSE PRACTITIONER

Mercy and data are
my rod and staff.
They comfort me.
Though naked I was born,
and feel so today,
and will be at the end of days,
I wrap myself in garments
inadequate to take this task.
The suffering, they labor for air.
I see their chests try to rise
from under hoses, tubes and lines.
Hospital corridors stretch out
into valleys of the shadow.
At the drive-through, I bend down
offering a nasal swab.
My gown resembles purity.
Each driver leans to their door sill,
looks up expectantly,
as if to seek communion at the rail.

COVID as a Parallel in May

The grass, the clouds, the blooming trees
attend their pace. The house stands plumb.

Progressions of a breath: Sparrows
cluster and disperse, cluster and disperse

along their morning rounds. And
raccoons wash their hands as usual.

The dog cocks her head more frequently
and guesses only you are out of place.

You vacillate. In sync, then out. At your
favorite bar, the wine glasses hibernate like bats.

Each plan, each action, macerates
in the pooling current of the calendar.

Even the frozen venison
you butchered in November waits,

waits for you to justify its sudden death.

Pandemic, 1918

1. France. Poppies blooming blood.

Hedged by four sheets strung on wire, my grandparents
spent their wedding night, December 1917:
a New York married-barracks, moans muffled,
the night before the men shipped out.
Three faces to a porthole on a transport ship.
Fish in a Barrel, riflemen would say, sometimes with pity.
Who would notice a patient in an Army hospital
with a different kind of cough?

2. Tennessee. Fields overflowing corn.

As a girl, my wife heard it from her grandfather.
Elmer could bear to tell it only once. He'd turned 18.
After morning chores he volunteered to bury rural dead.
A horse. A spade. One afternoon he rode up
to a silent farmhouse. The chicken gate was down.
The dogs had disappeared. He buried a family of six,
each at peace in their own proper bed.

3. Michigan. Orchards weighed with apples.

We socialize at a distance as he settles
on his grandmother, now passed.
She'd not forget at nine a wagon
daily coming past to load the dead.
Or the sight of her same-aged friend wrapped
in a sheet, a smaller bundle lifted on.

I imagine a stigma in her eye: something
she learned to see around, but never gone.
106, she died. Her breath disappeared as a bird
which glides silently beyond the trees.
She never did arrive at 2021,
with her narrow chest a heavy haul for air,
her voice a reed too thin to call her friend
when the wagon comes around again.

A Fable of Grain

A child seeks the raja out.

With but a grain of rice held out on a fingertip,
the child seeks to eat.

I ask only this. One grain doubled,
doubled again, on a chessboard every square.
The raja's not alarmed.
He sends a soldier out to get a loaded scoop.
Maybe a small pail, he calls out as an afterthought.

The seers concur the sky tomorrow
will be laced with blood.
Morning or evening? On that they disagree.

The child adds the grains, which overflow.
Then switches to an abacus, but it runs out of breath.
The stateroom doors stand swollen open soon enough.

The child calculates the toll. *How much?* the raja asks.
A grain of rice weighs but the sliver of a gram.

The child replies
From you? Five times the weight of
every plant and animal on earth.

The grain mutates into a cloud of mist:
just a sneeze. And this is just a fable.

Each day, a doubled swarm
grouts your breath until you suffocate.

The raja sums his harvest months,
his armies, and his confidantes.
How many buried is a later count.

What He Could Control of COVID

My physician friend Majid
took up santour,
his grandfather's instrument
graced across his lap.
He says it helps him contemplate

the slope of death. Before,
the old instrument sat propped
in the corner like an elderly relative
who's visiting: antique, passé.

Today my friend Majid began to play.
His initial notes? How awkward.
For now. But in full flight,
how eloquent the hammers, even to

their slender stalks and felted tips
as delicate as sparrow's legs. In time,
he'll play it for his children, to narrate
the century from the last great pestilence

to this.

Pandemic House Arrest

Last night my wife dreamt she stole a car.
A warning flag that
the walls the doors the windowpanes
confine our space without
the slightest give or grace.

Lacking traffic lights and white stripes
we don't signal lane changes anymore.
We weave we swerve
we drift onto the rumble strips
and no one's breathalyzing us.

Who knows if it's the final test,
this litmus of contentedness.
As she and I mesh ever closer,
will the friction of compacting gears
grind and shift to meld into a grift?

We negotiate what remains of space.
Until last night,
when she gunned a heisted Cadillac
straight through the crossroads
where she and I were meant to merge.

Consequence I

What You Said About Me

The first two sips of beer are the best,
you tease good-naturedly
as we huddle
on a second date
—the dark eddy
of a railway station bar.

First, foam annoys the upper lip.
Then bubbles bristle in the throat.
On brew, the stomach bloats.
But, oh, those first two draughts.

A river of passengers flows by,
head-on toward destinations, delays,
side-tracks, cancellations.
How we like to overlay our futures
onto those of passersby,
guessing at their plunges into rapids,
cascades, often jutting rocks,
hoping for a pool of calm.
How are they a match, you laugh.

A season on, and
now you banter with me smilingly.
Maybe this is more like wine,
slow to unfold complexity
in the us we're tasting every day.

At the Pedestal of Michelangelo's *David*

From where I stand his feet are huge,
his torso of desire
rippling up like solid smoke.
His head, made massive by its curls,
recedes two stories above.
All perspective, so they claim.

Michelangelo glimpsed the man-boy
asleep inside Carrera marble.

The sculptor must stand back
to better see the whole,
then approach again to lay on hands,
only to withdraw once more. Who doesn't
dance with spatial harmony?
—After all, your stylist leans away often
to survey your troubled hair—

The unviewed David
slowly limbs himself
from unveined rock.

We in the museum
have been gifted centuries
to converge around
his face's hive of golden ratios,
the way his arms and legs
balance in the asymmetric tension

of an idle pose.
A body ache sublime
as fresh figs covered in honey.

Gaunt, but Fresh in Love

Divorce triggers deprivation,
you explained.
Food's available. Just not for me.
And twenty-five was more
than you could spare.

In your walk, you'd lost
the confidence of dance.

I arrived by accidental glance.
You'd even fallen sick,
you in that blue kerchief,
hair hanging limp.
I looked past
shadows pooling in your cheeks,
your temple bones laid almost bare.
But hope's a gill net.
It gathers tides of yearnings
schooling through unreal light
beneath the surface.

I applied oils and honey
to the marks he left on you:
the broadside volley of a turned back,
each pinch-and-twist fiction
on your lack of wit,
his burlap comments
abrading your satin
into sexlessness.

By summer's end I washed your hair
as often as you wished.
And then you fed us both.

An Afternoon in the Smokies

I say it started
up at Alum Cave Bluff.
The woman,
later my wife,
and I, on a blanket
an hour's hike beyond
the last trail fork.
She drew me to the edge
to realize this:
as the sun proceeds,
the mountains and
their laps of ridges and valleys
fold, unfold, refold
shadow and light
light and shadow,
across dense leafy textures
progressing
always to a new illumination.
We two alone,
she eased me forward
enough to see everything
laid right in front of us.

My Lucky Jacket

My lucky jacket drapes me pleasingly:
a cross between the wings of victory
and an asbestos fire suit.
A cloth talisman,
it buffs my confidence
to polished brass.
After all, I wore it
during our initial kiss.
It's my fabric shield
the eyes of trolls roll off.
On my motorcycle, in the rain,
this jacket wards me
from a lightning strike.

You're my loving skeptic.
You claim it's not a coffin or a cure.
You claim what counts,
familiar or familial,
will rise within my skin.

My lucky jacket? Maybe
it's a rescue blanket made of foil:
shiny and appealing,
looking larger than it is,
but vanishingly thin
and less than lucky after all.

Strawberries

Red raspberries lie velvet at the mouth
but smaller than your kiss.

Astringent skin wraps blueberries.
Your quick kiss embittered
by my accidental slight?

Blackberries?
A cobbled tartness not your style.

But here today you looked for me.
You tied the tails of your shirt
to scoop an overspill of strawberries.

When you reminded me
of what's in season still,
we ran back to the garden,
grabbing handfuls up
to blossom on our lips.

Summer Sunday Volleyball

From the far side of the net,
I watch you leap
to tap the ball.
I observe an athlete,
her tee-shirt
riding up at every jump,
and I see the perfect navel
glance out momentarily,
the small mouth
of a cowrie shell set vertically.

How appealing, this attraction
centered in the muscles of the belly,
the ones you've worked so taut and tan.
Two Springs ago, you invited me
to drink from this narrow slipper
so your fever could recede.

Tuesday, you tell me you are pregnant.

Complicit as I am,
I'll learn to love by twice
the lace-like patterns
on your abdomen.
I should have known,
of all the money, love, and time
we'll offer up,
you'd launch your body first
into the sacrifice.

Pursuit of Food

The sea breathes restlessness
onto the rocks
as we toss lobster shells
into a scooping surf.

I pursue you through the food
I introduce to you.
You seem to like
the indirect approach.

Steamed clams in melted butter?
Try it with your fingers,
I suggest.
The taste of sunlight poured
through summer leaves.
No, you insist.
More like the time
we drew into
that first delicious kiss.

Sometimes,
as a meditative task,
I forage oysters
in the brackish flats.
There's odd comfort in the way
my rubber boots suck out
a path through eel's mud.
Not grounded, yet free
from being almost stuck.

I offer what I'm able to.
You tease me with
Whose food isn't both
the message and the messenger?
I won't deny. You famish me.
Let's start with finger food.

Power Outage

While in a book, my sight goes black. I start
to glide familiar walls with fingertips,
hearing your voice above the banister.
The dark air clings to me. I float to touch

the kitchen hutch. Creeping inside its drawer
my fingers lift a candle, strike a match.
Air against flicker strains it on the wick.
To keep it steady, my palm cups the light.

Chiaroscuro for what's intimate:
face, curl of hand, the fluid flame.
What's seen past my reach? Nearby walls contract,
and corners of our favorite rooms withdraw.

The hallway stretches. Floorboards arc away.
Melt wax sputters like a surprised whisper.
You trace your way downstairs. Reflected off
my eyes, the elongated yellow flame

might make them seem like cat's. And did you say
our first illusions still abide in us?
Almost invisible, your nightgown flows,
a liquid veil around your curtained limbs,

but for your pale hand sliding the vague rail.
The same light touch once found my bounding pulse,
back when I couldn't keep my eyes away.
How flush you seemed with light. I couldn't catch

the subtle shadow play. Then you demurred,
said *Save some for another day.* You knew,
as I did not, the contour of desire,
if fully lit, will lose its mystery.

Memoir

At first, we ricocheted
with every kind of play.
Hours strewn like clothes. Until
a draft notice cleaved our marriage bed.

On an aircraft carrier off Vietnam,
sheets stifled me at night,
wound around a canvas bunk.
Through the bulkhead, I heard
the ocean rushing past,
its constant gurgle
like declarations of the drowning.
Your letters wove and unwove the news.
That five word promise at the end
I read again, again.

Two men below decks
got in a broken-bottle fight one night.
My shirt and trousers stank of jet fuel
from bombing runs around the clock.

On my return, I touched your hands
as if they might fly away.
The kitchen window
sifted light around your silhouette.
I strained, afraid of that
which might refract. But no.
        You said you'd given up your body

for our nursing child,
you'd give your body up for me.

It took weeks,
but in the faint light of night
you mouthed progressions of my name
until one pillow took the place of two.

Athlete

He once dated an athlete
whose soul and body merged.

No dichotomy.
He could tell it in her gait,
her voice, her face.

Her favorite position
meant Center Forward.
He counted trophies
on a shelf above her bed.

All confluence,
decisions wrapped
in quick response,
she'd trigger
torso, thighs, arms:
kick on goal,
sliding tackle,
header in the net.

Back at her place
he could see
in her casual nudity
the muscled flexibility
of full intent.

She coached him
on the elevated skills:

Before you bend it in the net,
first play the touch pass
as we read each other's eyes.

A Meditation on My Wife, with Edith Piaf

As she sews,
the sounds of Edith Piaf
spill small white feathers
out the summer windowsills.
They filter through the garden shade
where I am troweling in
transplants from the woods.
I cannot see her,
smell her, hear her.
Enough that music brushes
past her as it flows.

What rivets my attention?
Occasionally she poses
as the other woman
in that unctuous dress
and low-slung voice:
accessories she stole
from someone
I never sought.

The Perfect Kiss

Your perfect kiss
                    —though loving—
isn't quite, she comments to me.
You took more care to learn the violin.
A cool mark laid among the crumbs
and crumpled napkins of a lunch.

Her former husband—the painter—
did not apply
                    a brushstroke touch,
and she'll not tolerate another
endless laying on
                    impasto
with a palette knife.

Now, she and I huddle over lunch.
Some days, our floating
                    permanence
clings to the broken mast of a bed
as much as anyone's.
Again,
her casual voice insists
the prelude opens on a minor key,
                    lentissimo:
the perfect kiss.

Romance Novel Cover Model

I'm the one who brings on ripples in a pond.

Irish Chieftain?
   Sure, I'll dress in green homespun.

Rugged Cowboy?
   I'll wince convincingly as she bathes my wound.

New York Fireman?
   The heat from photo lamps makes me glow.

My pumped physique is flash,
the bright shiny thing
that draws her to the low doorway
of a Scottish cottage, disheveled and in need,
her hair an avalanche, her skin teasing the light
along the edge of a strained chemise.

I never know for sure.
Do I just bring them to the threshold?
Or do I carry them across, as they dissolve
into the yes of their favorite scenario?

As for my wife,
I know what does the trick.
I'll don my pirate pants, my damn red sash
and let her catch me
bending over folding laundry.

Her Mother's Daughter

If you leave me
some notion of yourself,
what will it be?

A photo from a working trip?
You, next to a charred tank
on the battlefield.

Or that voicemail
in your reporter's voice,
as you stitch a naked narrative
I mistook for threads of mist?

I found a hair of yours
lying like the curve of a cello.
A resonance in absence.

When I hold our baby daughter,
at first she nestles to my chest.
Then she plants her hands
to raise her bobbling head,
eyes fixed on what I cannot see.

Massachusetts Colonial
Farmhouse Auction

My mother, in a steal, bought a hodge-podge box
to nab the Chinese jacket folded on the top.

Under it, an antique map of Ipswich,
four gilded teacups,
a thumb-rubbed tape measure,
twelve signed books—no volume two—,
ribbon-bound postcards in a delicate hand,
one human skull.
A blind plumb line into family.

She handed me, at nine, the skull.
You might get something out of this.

I never wondered
what its empty eyes had seen,
what tastes had cloyed to its palate,
how blood might have uncoiled
in its temples on a wedding night.
If it kissed as bride or groom
or if at all, did not occur to me.
What had the absent brain blurted
to the missing limbs in dire emergency?
Was its origin Aegean Sea? Tonkin Gulf?
Or simply Buzzard's Bay?

I peered into the nasal cavity,
its paper-thin scrolls of turbinates

once written with a history of perfume.
I stared into sockets, oblivious of
when I'd be staring back.

To most boys, life continues like the tides,
and I dandled it, a discard,
a lobster's molted shell. Now

the skull sits propped between Dickinson and Poe,
its imperturbability extended sixty years.
But what I've learned most
is what lay inside my mother's wry smile
as she handed it to me.

Photographic Portrait, Rural Tennessee, Circa 1895.

My wife's ancestral family sits
under trees in the sepia farmyard.
A rail fence cross-stitches
behind all seven:
Mama, Papa, Verna, Garland,
Mattie, Ina and the baby.
We know who's who
by nineteenth century penmanship
angled above each head.
Except the baby's.

The children, all under seven,
dress in pure-of-spirit white.
Curious, the baby sits up
without help.
And without a name.

Mama's lips compress
a tired attempt to smile.
Papa's eyes fixate forward,
his brow pale,
his lower face like rust on iron.
The children are expressionless
and straight as church.

With each birth, the shadow of the angel
shakes its rattle outside on a branch,
then sifts through rippled windowpanes

to abide in the infant's bedding.
No choice but to let the shadow pass.
Only then do they bestow a name,
usually when winter's gone.

1981, and Ina, ninety-two,
in the smooth-worn gingham
of work succored by scripture
hears Ross our infant
squall from his bassinet.
I rise to comfort him.
It wants to be held,
she casually remarks.

Becoming One Flesh with
Her Family History

My wife and I, when alone,
sometimes speak
an Appalachian tongue
turned up from spores in soil
among the half-collapsed
tobacco barns.

In speech, we trace out
her Orion,
fixed at night among the slopes.

Beyond East Tennessee
it's what family she's got,
our way of raising Ina Bell again
to school us
in the rhythm of a parable.

Our syntax is a dove-tailed box
packed with antique tools
whose use is honed
by our repeated handiwork.

But only when alone.

Never near a boss.
Or in a coffee shop.
And always at arms-length

from the neighborhood watch,
whose four-way stops articulate
but smooth suburban curves.

Consequence II

How Old Family Stories Go

Hard. A little shrunk.
Revealed with a flourish
on the cutting board,
a cured and hanging ham,
one of several,
drawn from a dark larder in the back
of a paid-down clapboard house.

Each time, descendants of the first cook
warm to their preferred culinary arts:
de-bone, carve, shave, mince.
Yet, somehow it grows.

Gesticulations plate the serving.
Pauses lend the character of sauce.
The chef in residence
presents a mouthful. Even so,
it's hard to chew.
Mostly, you've got to swallow whole
something you may digest for years.

My Veteran of Iraq

Two nights ago, at 29,
his heart collapsed, four years out of Iraq.
Next week, we'll cluster at the family plot.
My sister sobs she wasn't born
to clutch a folded flag.

In war, with mangled vehicles,
mechanics strip the intact parts.
Fuel pump, clutch, perhaps an axle,
roof hatch, carburetor, random gauges,
a machine gun mount.
Whatever works.

Back home in Pinson
Tennessee, he heard cicadas,
their constant whine
a band-saw through his head.

A jobless drift. Punctuated by
a chair he battered, now out on the curb,
hemmed between two garbage cans.
A son meandering inside the fence
around the yard.
Tremors in his eyes
when he tried to talk to us.

Meth: a gnashing chatter.
Heroin: molasses in a moan.

His Purple Heart
next to its recovered bullet
in a satin-lined box.

A year of VA rehab lockdown,
with a Johnson City keyhole view:
his line of sight lost in the mountains
from a bench out on the lawn.

His heart collapsed two nights ago
at 29. Now, he's on life support
until they harvest organs.

Black Baby Doll

I was six, my sister three.
A western Massachusetts farm.
Red barn angles. Roundstone walls
heaved into balance by
such diversity as Dutch,
Norwegians, French, Finns,
a smattering of Greeks.

Christmas, and outside
was a heaved-up sea of white,
silent, motionless.

As a gift for Natalie,
a Black baby doll
in its snowy tissue paper crèche.
New rubbery smell, glassy gaze,
short dark hair, pudge fingers.
Especially
its fresh mocha skin
in pink baby doll pajamas.
We peered and peered, heads touching,
hands sniffing like country mice.
Bemused, our mother watched
without a word.

She knew we had never seen
someone Black.
James Baldwin would have to

smoke another pack
before we found him lounging
on her bookshelf in our teens.

Lobstering at 96

The greasy swells are out today. Tides tie my schedule,
half-adrift upon her death last year.

My skin sprouts barnacles and mats of kelp. So thin
it tears against a tightened line. Bruises spread

like algae blooms in blue. Whips of salt spume toughen
even skinny boys. She married to unpeel me the man. Today,

I combed her plot with care. What with the cemetery poorly kept,
my friends might well be buried in a vacant lot. My neighbors are

their sprat. They strut like gulls, innocent of history.
Not the blizzard of '50 when every boat and car

was clamped in ice three weeks, the sea a sullen gray,
and half the fishing shacks were pick-up sticks.

The warmer weather is a weakling nowadays. Between
sinews and my knobby joints, these limbs resemble

knotted rope. Still, I had to haul the pots. The sea, and she,
are all I care to know. I learned eddies from flow,

surface from undertow. My jury is the clouds, the sun,
the wind. Lobsters molt. July's their naked month, but

I'll not be reborn. With her, one long visit to the county fair was plentiful. And she won't meet me at the gate again.

I'll be grateful when I shed my shell this once.

A Study of My Wife Cutting My Hair

She plants her palm
on top of my head
as though she would
a cantaloupe.
Sharp work wants close control.

My hair is not my glory. Carry on.

Her focus is a form of solitude,
unreachable to me, yet still,
still, so close to her skin
I can smell the lotion
she applied last night.

How often I forget,
until five weeks from now,
again, she sets her palm
atop my head,
a blessing of this union,
a promise of this pact.

Violin

Asymmetry's an attribute,
you and I were soon to learn.

The bow hand meant for tempo,
the other hand fingering the tune.

In light and heavy frictions
of compression and release,
we play out brio,
we play out lentamente,
with equal fluency.

But sometimes,
as I near the top of the stairs,
or begin to fold a shirt,
or transit a glacial thought,

you emerge,
entirely congruent
with me, and again
I revel in something
like the mouth feel
of a bursting tangerine.

You take
your coffee black.
I don't.

Unexplained Weight Loss

First, she notices his face
in slants of light.
A narrowing. A melt.

One dawn a shoulder blade breaches
toward her in bed
as he turns to rise.

His skin grows pockets
where rainwater might collect.

The doctor equivocates
in a sawing motion
without a sentence stop.

Abrupt, his rib-like corrugations.

Familiar music from his tongue
fractures into sharps and flats.

She nurtures him with sex,
then lays his ungainly head,
a boulder, at her neck.
He senses not himself
but an illicit traveler wedged
between her skull and clavicle.

#MeToo—A Father Responds

Some hands grab for dirty work, up close.
So my daughter's pit bull runs with her at dawn.

My wind-worn wings can't span the sky.
For her sake, I want to be what's strange and terrible.
Osiris's black jackal would intercede. His job?
To drag the corpse of lust's assumptions underground.
To weigh its shriveled heart.
But could I recognize deceit seeping from the pores?
Maybe not. Pit bulls possess a better sense of smell.

A Sailor and the Contents of His Duffel Bag

Seafarers Who Die Left Aboard.

Washington Post, Nov 20, 2021.

I can hardly heave his body overboard,
much as I might wish.
Now I'm assigned pilot of this vessel
in a simple matter of seniority.
Our assemblage plows and heaves sea to sea.
A mostly long-term crew, a few who sign on and off,
inside a maze of passageways and rooms
with something of an engine underneath.
Like a family I suspect.

My mother gripped the helm for years
up on the bridge, desperate, strict.
She died of heart attack. At her request,
how dignified her burial at sea
while a cormorant inscribed the sky.
Her drunk second mate
staggered to command,
eyes like bloodshot quail's eggs.

He thought he'd last.

For now, I've wrapped and stashed
his body in the freezer
on a rack behind the beef and pork.

No port but his home port
will hoist him on their wharf.

I've recovered her captain's log
and unrolled her charts.
Her notes on shoals were written
during twenty years.

Some ships haul humanitarian aid.
Some pack cheap wine, guns, and pestilence.
Some breeze into port, their pennants high.
Some carry refugees
who pray only for the sight of land.

When the Steelers Play at Home

After mother's burial,
father-daughter talk resembled
a drive through blocks of steel towns:
facades in disrepair, interspersed with vacant lots.
She strains for a verb, a noun, a latch to catch.

> *Oh, look! Now there's a sale!*

> *Your mother used to shop there,*
> *Paula girl. See? "Everything must go"*

Sundays are his anesthesia
for a memory banked by dying coals .
Kickoff in the afternoon will steel his nerves.
A boiled kielbasa on the TV tray.
Eating without relish. Bathed in blue.

And Paula, swelled with motherhood,
adjusts her tray, lingers for an opening.
She views the knockdown game of inches,
averts her eyes from the slo mo crack back replay.

A new language is harder for adults.
Horse collar   hash marks   naked bootleg
flea flicker   wounded duck   split the uprights
alligator arms   jailbreak   laces out.

Mondays, she sips a mild tea
as her index finger pioneers the sporting news.

Roethlisberger, third and short?
Tight end on a crossing route I'll bet.

Paula girl, you got that right.
Mom always stirred up
cheese on chili for the half
then kissed me twice for luck.
Want to watch next week?

With a tight spiral off her front foot
she's found the open man.

Snapshot, Aleutian Islands, 1934

Gill-hooked on a chain,
a halibut
long as a dory
hangs from a bull pine's bough.
Wide as angled sails,
edged in fins, tail forked.
Its belly swell a swath
of white gloss.

My great-uncle, his wife,
and her gal friend
bask
in front of a season of food.
The women drape each other
loose as play.
Fists holding a meat hook,
he hoists a second halibut.
Uncut filets to lay out,
row on row on row.

Curing racks,
salt in buckets,
smokehouse,
knife, shovel, ax.

In the urban lower 48,
their heads bent away and down,
hidden by hats
from a photographer,

men stack themselves like
stood-up cords of wood.
For apples:
seeds, stems,
paltry flesh and skin.

Long Love Comes of Age

At last, slow toward the bed,
our Buddhist shrine.
But first we'll set offerings
on bedside tables: candles, pills, fruit,
additives, two glasses of water,
a favored lotion, emoluments of dusk.
The method of an operatic ritual.
Which will it be tonight? Consummation?
Or a lesser comfort equal to the need?
There's little anymore we can predict.

Punding

*The repetition of complex motor behaviors such as
collecting or arranging objects.*

It's working all of us, and all the time. Not just
as obvious obsessions with diagnostic names,
the car-horn ones you notice corralling someone else

as you avert your eyes. Don't be coy. Punding
hums to you and me. Collect. Arrange. My mother
took up figurines, blaming the Depression for her want.

Myself, I go by color, size, or function for my stuff.
The superego interrupts: *In this implicit way,
are you not sorting people with a glance?*

Rockport Graves

Both buried wives await his late arrival
at the open plot between.
A cordial plan. Who could complain?

    In its parlor, death sculpts
    something like her face in sallow clay.
    The husband whispers down
    I'll see you on a cloud.
    He'd murmured it once before.
    Caregiver. Caretaker. Undertaker. All.

They sit up to wait, playing cards
across his weightless coffin
hovering above the grass.
It's ultimate, this game of chance.
I drew a melanoma.
You discarded oral cancer,
but got left holding Alzheimer's.
They laugh about his hands,
comparing strokes.
They share another cigarette
with lipstick tints that match.
He likes consistency, you do recall.
Ash to ash when ghosts of smoke arise.

But the onward heart inhales
a passing conversation with a third:
a youngish widow from the club perhaps,
and the reel of time tightens up the line these days.

He likes her recipes.
She studies him like a final offer:
his methodology of socks,
how he'd lift her hair to whisper to her neck,
and how he'd be interred with her.

Meanwhile, playing cards,
waiting for a death by chance,
the two wives cannot realize how eternity,
like fanning out a hand of cards,
expands like an accordion.

A Mother, Sniper for Ukraine

Sometimes I'm a pile of leaves.
Other times a clump of underbrush.
Every Russian on patrol thinks
every moss-covered log is me.

You saw the photograph,
the world did too:
baby Oleg's face lopsided
as I plaster my kiss
against his cheek and
squeeze him, lingering.
Two days of leave
are not enough.

I am one with the ground
when mortar rounds
begin to fall nearby.
I can taste my country's soil
as it showers me.
You always smell like dirt,
the baby's father laughs.

He and I probe
the same contested villages:
chickens, dogs, rubble,
with a glance
at every foreign body.
We implore each other often,
Bury me properly.

I offered my train ticket out
to a ten-year-old boy.
I won't be buried
as a bent babushka
in Poland or America,
when all is calm and bright,
our farm rebuilt by someone else.

To My Father, Poet Carpenter

Must be the grain and how
it flows around the knot to re-convene.
Its smooth meanderings remind him
of his love of trees.

He runs his thumb along a finished edge,
his palm across a sanded flat.
Like butter, the iambic luster
of a tulip poplar plank.

His latest table keeps its shape with
four conjunctions and a pair of screws.
He dovetails different woods:
for instance
love and its attempted metaphor.

He leans into his routers
and his circular saws.
It's no surprise he lacks a fingertip.

Through the din,
my mother calls out suppertime,
but he won't stop as long as
his lips work a chalked line of verse,
and a sawdust of words
settles in his hair.

A Fenced-Off Quarry

My mother, in her teens, would sneak
up here with friends to swim.
No fence. No lock. No chain or gate.
But someone else's property, she knew.

As teenagers ourselves, we heard this story
several times: of her edging up at night
with her one-legged beau, how they skinny-dipped
in the moon's milk, voices hushed,

with probably a lot of untold making out
in the underbrush. All caress and giddiness, until
he couldn't find his artificial leg. The hobbling
and the whispering, the frantic search. And how

they had to sidle back the next day, to find it
at attention in a raspberry bush. By now,
father smirks and mother's eyes dart as if to say
you knew me when we wed. Years since,

I've swum up here a few times, after
ducking underneath the gate. A box-like
granite quarry, its cliffs, its hundred fathoms
looming underneath, its shock of chill

when diving off a ledge. Then I burnish
in the sun beside the wild shrubs. And
like a hawk forever overhead, a story with
the feathers of a myth, one fenced off and out of reach.

The Chain Saw and Its Vedic Dance

At times, sequestration seems the best.
To thin a copse of trees
I tug my plastic earmuffs on,
sponge plugs underneath,
with goggles and a sawdust mask.
I insulate. From two dogs
chapping down the lane,
a neighbor on her tractor driving off.

Immersion means a muffled roar,
reverberations of a blade across a grain,
a rooster tail of fragrant dust.
Between the warmth of work and sun
I move as if the day were drawn from honey.

My eyes dilate. My breathing calms.
The engine thrums its way
along my arms. Most of all
the space inside my chest pulsates,
a hollow hum in lungs and diaphragm:
vibrations of a meditative Om.

Amelia Earhart felt the plane
throughout her frame.
That's how it is
to dream of some machines.
Like the saw my father let me try
when I was ten,
his watchful hand extended

as I learned the dance,
its tension, its release.

Ironing Her Hair

Cletis had been missing half a finger
since the 1920s labor wars.
Blood brawls and sporadic work.
Then tenant farming dusk to dark.

What was attached
was her, a granddaughter of 15.
   A girl needs better than an absent father.
The old man taught her of the ways of dogs, of bulls,
of rams. Of swine and how they rip up sod
and how to pierce a steel ring through a hog's snout.
   He'll squeal at first. Then he'll settle down.
   And I keep my guard because each herd has a vicious one.
At first a flyaway girl in white Keds, she listened carefully.

Despite the TV's snowy interferences,
despite slim glimpses from network studios, still
she sought the black and white of broadcast marches.
Odetta, Pete Seeger,
the clapping of a mass in motion.

She funneled her thin self into Joan Baez,
dark waves spilling toward her waist.
   Pa-paw, will you iron my hair?
   I want it straight like hers.

He hesitated, not having ever ironed,
as she laid her head to the board's edge.
   I don't want to burn you, doodle-bug.

Resembling ancient oak roots,
his hands glided slowly,
in pace with her awakening.
Still, he took pains to warn her
of the beatings on a picket line.

Pica

Craving and chewing substances
that have no nutritional value

In pregnancy,
—all twelve of them—
my wife's grandmother recalled
she leaned over on her hoe
to pinch up fingerfuls of dirt to eat:
iron needed to firm her blood.

The fraught weather
of an iron sky.
The blackened iron frying pan.
The iron in her face toward
the front page president.

Compulsion weighed her
like a ninth-month backache.

Her husband and the bulk of working men?
They shifted through factories and rail yards
as the Depression coughed up
a sustenance like pica:
dirt, bones, chalk, paper, ash.

Midnight and the Veteran

About midnight,
I cradle my forehead
between your shoulder blades,
gradually, quietly,
since you are so at peace, asleep.

Shooting stars begin to fall,
then hiss like illumination flares,
swelling into tracer bullets
pocking up the dirt all around.
I dream your nephew Adam and I
are lost on patrol in Afghanistan.
But it can't be.
I'm still under rocket fire in Vietnam.
Where is the sapper who
can detonate these obstacles?

Then, to recover my body,
I hold you against me
for an hour,
yet you never wake.

Lifespan of a Bracelet

Eyes lined in kohl,
you wore the bracelet last night
to our favorite Turkish restaurant.
It shimmered under candlelight
as the grace of your bare arms
traced the ebb and flow
of a cello's notes.

Twenty years ago, I took
my pallid grandmother on my arm.
It was her last dodder into town.
She spotted
her similarly listing neighbor
down the street,
and in a gimlet voice
whispered, *Look
at how she's gone to seed.*

Even in her nineties,
in fly-away white hair,
how proud she was
she could show her ankle
thin and shapely.
*A perfect shape
and thin as well.*
Brusque as ever,
she gestured with her hand
as that same gleam of gold

slid up, then down
her mottled wrist.

An Impending Death

Supposedly I knew, due to
my own mother's death in rural Maine,
how to walk this mournful path,
its scrub, its tilted woods,
its moonless field.

I had wiped her mouth,
held her hand, a frail flightless bird,
changed her garment often
as though always getting ready for a trip.
She complied, not knowing me.

Two months before,
she persevered at one request:
to raise her to the window
to view the Irish Sea.
From its cliffs
jostles a sun-laced eternity.

After she died, I had to remember
the path back in the dark.

Now, my wife, in another state,
phones from her mother's hospice room,
and asks if I'd describe the route.

As a kitchen toddler, her small fingers
memorized a hem of gingham dress.

Memory mixed, her mother now insists
on that dress to travel in

toward a deep Tennessee forest
where leaves of scripture
flock in trees beyond the rail fence.

The Hospice Music Therapist

Oh my, I didn't mean to startle you.
I'm not the oarsman or the angel,
not the horseman, judge, or ancestor.
No, dear, I'm your music therapist,
a girl fresh out of grad school
here to sing your favorites.
Grasp my hand. My pulse is warm.
Now that makes two of us.
Me by your bed. You in it.

What music did you and your mother love?
Or your grandfather,
as his radio crackled in the dim garage?
By what song did you fall in love?
There's ever only one.

Sweetie, let me clear my voice.
I want to hit the high notes right for you.
My Funny Valentine
Ave Maria
Besa Me Mucho
Swing Low, Sweet Chariot
Some even need a lullaby.

Music is a river indivisible,
lyrics a vee of geese that lands,
to depart, to land again along the flow.

It's happened only once
as a woman breathed her last.
She drifted on my final stanza
as I sang her from this world.

Acknowledgments

Ponder Review:

"Hanging by a Thread" (published as "Spit into the Cup")

Poetry Virginia Review:

"Meditation on Gregor Mendel"

"Unexplained Weight Loss"

Artemis:

"To You, Mary Shelley"

The Poetry Box:

"Aching for an Oracle" (published as "Saliva Test")

"That Punk Look"

"Raining Diamonds"

"Athlete"

"When the Steelers Play at Home"

"The Chainsaw and its Vedic Dance"

Streetlight

"Pandemic, 1918"

"First Sonogram"

"How Family Stories Go"

"Punding"

Superpresent:

"After My Cousin Posted Her DNA"

"The Perfect Kiss"

"Her Mother's Daughter"

Café Review:

   "To the Next Cold Case Killer"

   "Free Heroin"

   "Narcan"

Journal of The American Medical Association:

   "On a Surgeon Poet"

The Northern Virginia Review:

   "After Watching the History Channel with You"

   "A Neat Trick if You Can"

   "Power Outage"

Zeotrope:

   "Under the Influence of Internet"

Poetrywithmathematics.blogspot.com:

   "Police Will Swab Your Cheek"

   "A COVID Fable"

But Does It Rhyme:

   "Gene Silencing"

   "An Impending Death"

NoVaBards:

   "Zipper"

Alpha Female Society:

   "What the Eye Perceives"

The Sow's Ear:

   "Song Stuck in Your Head"

Fictional Café:

    "What You Said About Me"

    "Pursuit of Food"

    "An Afternoon in The Smokies"

    "A Study of My Wife While Cutting Hair"

    "Violin"

    "Gaunt, But Fresh in Love"

    "My Lucky Jacket"

    "After a Summer Hike"

    "A Meditation on My Wife, with Edith Piaf"

    "Summer Sunday Volleyball"

The Journal of Neurology:

    "Falling Asleep"

Poetry Society of Virginia 2020 Anthology:

    "AJ and the Chipper"

    "Massachusetts Colonial Farmhouse Auction"

    "To My Father, Poet Carpenter"

Poetry Society of Virginia newsletter:

    "To the Healthcare Workers"

The Writer's Center:

    "COVID as a Parallel in May"

Global Poemic:

    "What He Could Control of COVID"

Joys of The Table Anthology:

    "Strawberries"

    "Snapshot, Aleutian Islands, 1934"

Throats to the Sky:

"Memoir"

Burningword:

"My Iraqi Veteran"

Passager:

"Lobstering at 96"

"Midnight and the Veteran"

Arlington County Transportation Dept:

"#MeToo—A Father Responds"

Poetry Society of Virginia 2023 Anthology:

"Lifespan of a Bracelet"

"A Mother, Sniper for Ukraine"

The Imaginative Conservative:

"First, the Good News"

First Place Prizes from the Poetry Society of Virginia
2014, Edgar Allen Poe Memorial Prize

"Under the Influence of Internet"

2016, Charlotte Wise Memorial Prize

"Unexplained Weight Loss"

2019, Nancy Byrd Turner Memorial Prize

"A Meditation on Gregor Mendel"

2023, Brodie Herndon Memorial

"A Mother, Sniper for Ukraine"

2023, Charlotte Wise Memorial Prize

"Lifespan of a Bracelet"